Mona Wilson

Our Industrial Laws

Working women in factories, workshops, shops and laundries, and how to help

them

Mona Wilson

Our Industrial Laws
Working women in factories, workshops, shops and laundries, and how to help them

ISBN/EAN: 9783743407695

Manufactured in Europe, USA, Canada, Australia, Japa

Cover: Foto ©ninafisch / pixelio.de

Manufactured and distributed by brebook publishing software
(www.brebook.com)

Mona Wilson

Our Industrial Laws

OUR INDUSTRIAL LAWS.

Working Women in Factories, Workshops, Shops and Laundries, and How to Help Them.

OUR INDUSTRIAL LAWS.

WORKING WOMEN IN FACTORIES,

WORKSHOPS, SHOPS AND LAUNDRIES, AND

HOW TO HELP THEM

BY MONA WILSON

EDITED, WITH A PREFACE, BY

MRS. H. J. TENNANT

[ISSUED BY THE INDUSTRIAL LAW COMMITTEE.]

LONDON

DUCKWORTH & CO.

3, HENRIETTA STREET, COVENT GARDEN, W.C.

1899.

PREFACE.

Although it is hoped that this book may be of use to any one interested in our Industrial Laws, it is principally designed to meet the needs and answer the questions of persons who are in a position to make the administration of these laws effective. Prominent among those so qualified by their position are District Visitors, Deaconesses, Mission Workers, Residents in Settlements, Helpers in Friendly Societies and Working Girls' Clubs; and it is in answer to a desire widely expressed to the Industrial Law Committee that the book has been written: in answer to a desire for a fuller knowledge of the laws which govern the industrial conditions of our workers in factories and workshops, that by the aid of such knowledge practical service may be given to them in some of the most pressing and directive circumstances of their life. For the conditions in the factory or workshop are often governing elements in the conditions of the home, which they serve to guide and mould even when they do not directly control. The work-place claims most of the waking hours of the day; there is little time left when the day's work is done for leisure and its uses of recreation and improvement ; there is little time left in which to counteract the influence, if it be a bad influence, of the factory day.

It, therefore, is matter with grave bearing upon the work of all whose concern is the welfare of working women and girls that the conditions of their working life are those ordained by the law. It is intended in the Factory and Workshop Acts, in the Public Health Acts, and in the Truck Acts, to provide for safety, health and morals, for the just discharge of wages contracts, and to give general protection from oppression by unjust fines or deductions. In the Employers' Liability. Act, and by the Workmen's Compensation Act, it is intended to supplement the Common Law and provide compensation in cases of injury or death by accident, to the injured worker or his family. And upon the administration of these laws which touch and control their working life, depends in great measure the economic, social and moral welfare of the nation's workers.

The social workers to whom I have referred, who are in intimate relationship with the conditions which cry out for relief, are those who can most easily judge of the depth and extent of the injury, and who can most easily apply the remedy. On the one hand they can see the injury to health if excessive hours are worked; if meal times are not observed; if the workplace be ill-warmed or ill-ventilated, or otherwise insanitary; or if a " dangerous " trade be carried on

without due precaution; the cruel injury to limb and
life if dangerous machinery be unguarded; the injustice
to children and to their future if health or education be
stunted by employment at too early an age or by neglect
of the legal educational requirements ; the degrading
influence upon the moral tone in a factory if the sanitary
accommodation offend against the decencies of life ; the
injustice of fraudulent miscalculation and the consequent
reduction of the wages agreed upon, and its effect upon
the wage-earning power of the household ; the constant
injustice—again bearing the same harmful effect, of
. fines and deductions ; and the hardship of the sudden
withdrawal of a wage-earner, killed or injured at his
employment, without even compensation in money to
those who were dependent upon him for their daily bread.
On the other hand, there is the law, and a body of
Inspectors to enforce it.   The task of bringing the law to
bear upon the wrong, of bringing the Inspectors to the
relief of those who are oppressed, is one of justice and
of mercy; that it may be made simple is the object of
this book and of the Industrial Law Committee, and
that this object may be the better fulfilled, I venture to
suggest the following matters as points it is well to
keep in view when noting conditions of work :—

    1. The information should be as detailed and as
accurate as possible.

    2. The name and address of the work-place

should be clearly given; the address should include, where possible, the number or name of the building which contains the work-place, and when it is one of others in a common building the floor should be stated.

3. The name and address of the person who forwards the information should be stated (*not for publication in any form*) either to the Industrial Law Committee or to the Authorities. This is very necessary in order to facilitate further enquiry, and it is often desirable, though not perhaps necessary, that the Inspector should be in possession of the name of the original informant or of the worker on whose behalf representation is made. As the degree of desirability and usefulness varies according to the nature of the matter complained of, and as, in some cases, the possession of such knowledge may be wholly unnecessary, it is advisable if the workers be at all reluctant, not to disclose their names, though it is most desirable to inspire them generally with confidence in the discretion and good faith of the Inspectors.

4. When representation is made about cases of overwork or breach of meal hours it is especially important to give careful details of the situation of the room or department complained of, if it be one of others in the same building. Alarm may

be spread and detection therefore evaded by the Inspector's entry of a room on the first floor in search of work which is proceeding perhaps on the fifth floor, and which is speedily discontinued at the note of alarm. By aid of the detailed information which I have indicated such a case can be made impossible. Everything should be stated for the benefit of the Inspector, which will facilitate, 1st, rapid entry of the premises, and 2nd, rapid entry of the special room. In those workshops where a system of signals prevails for the evasion of the Factory Inspector, measures to ensure rapid entry are absolutely essential to success. Where also the system prevails of concealing workers in bedrooms, or when it has been threatened or is suspected, the Inspector should be informed.

5. It is important to ascertain if the Abstract of the Factory and Workshop Acts be exhibited, if it contain the proper entries of meal times, times of starting and leaving off work, &c., &c., and if it be hung up in a suitable place *where it can be easily read*. It must not be defaced, or concealed by other papers or by patterns.

6. It is also of importance to ascertain whether in places where overtime is worked the conditions are properly observed; whether entry is duly made

of each occasion of overtime in the proper official form, *before such overtime is begun.*

7. In representations about matters of sanitation care should be taken to state, if possible, the degree of defect complained of, *e.g.*, if the accommodation be considered insufficient, its extent in relation to the number of persons employed; or if it be considered otherwise unsuitable, the degree and nature of its unsuitability. Notice of sanitary defects in workshops, if not sent through the Industrial Law Committee, should be sent to the Medical Officer of Health for the District.

8. One of the most beneficial sections in the Act of 1895 is that which requires the maintenance of a reasonable temperature in workrooms. Where the law is infringed and the workers complain of extreme cold, it is well to ascertain whether, as is sometimes the case, the temperature is raised at a certain period of the day by the lighting of a fire, by gas, or by other means. Should this be so it is useful to inform the Inspector, in order that the visit may not be accidentally paid at the moment when the temperature is reasonable.

9. If complaint be made by the workers of dangerous machinery in a factory or a laundry, it is well to ascertain if its unfenced state has been the cause of accident, and to mention, if possible, the

date and nature of the accident, the name and address of the injured person, and whether he or she be still unable to attend work. The requirement placed upon employers to report accidents is not always observed, and it may be of considerable importance to the injured person that his accident should be made known to the Factory Department. A penalty of £100 is recoverable from an employer for failure to fence dangerous machinery by which injury or loss of life has been caused, and the sum recovered may be applied to the injured worker or his family by the Secretary of State. This provision has often proved of value in cases where a worker, through ignorance, poverty, or fear of consequences would otherwise have remained entirely without compensation ; and it is well, therefore, to bear in mind its possibilities. But the greatest opportunities for compensation are afforded under the special compensation laws, and the Industrial Law Committee are indebted to Mr. Alfred Lyttelton for his kind preparation of the following suggestions as to the circumstances which should determine the course to be pursued and the Act under which proceedings should be taken :—

A workman employed in a dangerous trade (*i.e.*, in factories, mines, etc.), when injured in accidents arising out of and in the course of his employment, will, in the majority of cases, avail himself of the remedy provided by the Workmen's Compensation Act of 1897. His sole obligation is to prove before the tribunal prescribed by the Act—

(I.) 1. That the accident happened.

2. That it arose out of and in the course of the employment.

3. The damage resulting to him.

4. To negative any allegation that the accident was due to his (the workman's) wilful misconduct.

He himself or any fellow-employé may have been careless, and so caused the accident; pure misadventure may have caused it; the employer and all connected with him may have been wholly free from blame; yet the workman, if he satisfies the four conditions set out above, is absolutely entitled to compensation under the scale provided by the Act.

(II.) In cases of serious injury—that is to say, in cases where a jury may be safely expected to give £100 or more—the workman, if he can afford it, should consult a lawyer, whether his case is within the Employer's Liability Act, 1880, and whether by proceeding under that Act he is likely to recover considerably more than under the Act of 1897. The intricacy of the Act of 1880 is so great that to summarise it popularly would be simply misleading. It should, however, be noted that a workman must

consult a lawyer sufficiently soon to enable notice of
the accident to be given to his employer within six
weeks of the occurrence of the accident.

(III.) A third remedy, at Common Law, is open
to an injured workman, even if his employment be not
in a dangerous trade, against his employer. If the
injury has been caused by the direct personal negligence
or wrongdoing of the employer himself, as dis-
tinguished from the negligence or wrongdoing of any of
his subordinates, the workman may recover against him
in an action an indemnity not bounded by any
statutory limit, and in bad cases a jury is entitled
to give even "vindictive damages"—*i.e.*, such a sum
of money as will represent not merely indemnity
to the workman but a penalty on the offending
master. To adopt this form of remedy rather
than that prescribed in the Workmen's Compensation
Act of 1897 is a step of such gravity that no sensible
workman ought to take it, unless (1) the injuries
he has sustained are very serious and the compensation
recoverable largely exceeding that which he could obtain
under the Act of 1897 ; and (2) unless he is advised by a
competent lawyer to do so. For many defences—*e.g.* (1)
contributory negligence, (2) knowledge of, and apprecia-
tion by, the workman of the risks involved, (3) negligence
of a fellow-workman, (4) mishap or misadventure—are
available to the employer in such an action which are

not available under the Workmen's Compensation Act
of 1897.   No prudent workman should then proceed
under the Common Law or the Employer's Liability
Act of 1880 without competent professional advice, and
the expense of taking that advice should not be incurred
unless the preliminary conditions already mentioned in
II. and III. are satisfied.

It must, however, be observed that if a workman
brings an action under II. or III. and fails, the Court
shall, if required, assess compensation under the Act of
1897, and has a discretion to deduct from such compensation all the costs thrown away by the abortive
proceedings.   This discretion will and ought to be used
unless a case has been presented which establishes the
good faith and reasonableness of the plaintiff.

————

It has not been considered advisable to give in the
text an account of the regulations which relate to docks,
building operations or other matters which are not likely
to come under the notice of those for whom the book is
intended.   These regulations are fully stated in the
larger book of reference, to which readers of this book
are referred.   For a similar reason the " Special Rules "
which govern " Dangerous " Trades are not given ; they
are given at length in " The Law relating to Factories
and Workshops," or the rules for each trade can be
obtained separately, at the cost of about 1d., from
Messrs. Eyre & Spottiswoode.   But although the

inclusion of all the rules would probably have over-weighted the book for those in whose districts no "dangerous" trades are carried on, I believe it will be of value to make known the industries to which " Special Rules" have up to now been applied, and I give therefore the following list. Anyone who is interested in the welfare of workers who are engaged in a certified "dangerous" trade should become acquainted with the "Special Rules" which govern employment in that trade, and ascertain if they are observed by the firm and by the workers themselves.

Bichromate Works.

Bottling of Aerated Water.

Brass and Alloys, Mining and Casting.

Chemical Works.

Earthenware and China Manufactories.

Electric Accumulator Works.

Enamelling of Iron Plates.

Explosive Manufactories (where di-nitro-benzole is used).

Flax Spinning and Weaving Works.

Lead (red and orange) Works.

Lead (white) Works.

Lead (yellow) Works.

Lead Smelting Works.

Lead (yellow chromate of) Works, where used.*

---

* Principally used in Print and Dye Works.

Lucifer Match Factories (where white or yellow phosphorus is used).

Paint and Colour Manufacture and Extraction of Arsenic.

Tinning and Enamelling of Iron Hollow Ware.

Tinning and Enamelling of Metal Hollow Ware and Cooking Utensils.

Vulcanising Indiarubber by means of bisulphide of carbon.

Wool and Hair Sorting.

In the suggestions as to the form in which information should be prepared for Inspectors I have not attempted to deal with all the cases of complaints which are likely to arise. I have endeavoured only to illustrate the general importance of attention to detail, and to suggest the kind of explicit statement which will enable the Inspectors to deal most promptly and effectively with the infringements of the law which present the greatest difficulties of detection, and which will sometimes spare them unnecessary visits to employers whose houses are already in order.

The fear and ignorance which prevail among many of the workers time, kindly teaching and sympathy alone can break down. This sympathy is already articulate— it has been given expression in many ways ; and its full force will, I believe, be gained when there comes with it the recognition of the deeper meaning of factory life and of its bearing upon the life of the home and of the nation. A charter of protection is within grasp, but its benefits are often lost to those who need them most : they do not know, or, knowing, they dare not claim. And those who stand by their side seeking opportunities of service, have in their turn this opportunity given them by a merciful law of bringing light and health and justice to lives encaged in poverty, dimmed and scarred by suffering, embittered by wrong.

MAY TENNANT.

CONTENTS.

NOTES ON REFERENCES.

"The Law Relating to Factories and Workshops," by May E. Abraham and A. Llewelyn Davies, published by Eyre and Spottiswoode, is quoted only as "Law Relating to Factories and Workshops." The edition referred to is the Second Edition.

In almost all cases, the forms and documents required to be kept under the Factory and Workshop Acts are prescribed by the Secretary of State, and the prescribed forms only may be used. For simplicity, the word "prescribed" does not accompany every reference to the Abstract, Overtime Record, &c., but its use may be understood.

OUR INDUSTRIAL LAWS.

CHAPTER I.

FACTORIES AND WORKSHOPS.

BEFORE entering on the requirements of the Factory and Workshop Acts, it is important to note the difference between a factory and a workshop. Those work-places in which mechanical power is used are defined as factories. Other work-places in which no power is used are defined as workshops, with the exception of a few which are specially included among the non-textile factories.[1]

There are some further distinctions which cannot be overlooked even in the most general survey of the law.

TEXTILE AND NON-TEXTILE.—Factories are divided into textile and non-textile. The former are,

2

with certain exceptions, factories in which processes connected with the manufacture of wool, hair, silk, flax, etc., are carried on.   All others are non-textile.[2]

DIFFERENT CLASSES OF WORKSHOPS.— Three special kinds of workshops are on a different footing from the ordinary workshop:—

(1.) Domestic workshops, where the employés are members of one family, all dwelling in the same house in which the work is carried on.[3]

(2.) Workshops from which children and young persons are excluded.

(3.) Workshops in which men only are employed.[4]

PERSONS EMPLOYED.—The Acts differ in their application for the various classes of persons employed:—

(1.) Adult men whose hours of labour are in no case directly regulated by the Factories and Workshops Acts.

(2.) Women.

(3.) Young persons—*i.e.*, boys and girls between 14 and 18.   A child of 13 who has an Educational Certificate ranks as a young person ; the Certificate must state (*a*) that Standard V. has been passed, or (*b*) that the qualifying number of attendances have been made.[5]

(4.) Children between 11 and 14.   No child under 11 may be employed in a factory or workshop.

NOTICES.—In every factory and workshop (with the exception of domestic workshops) the abstract of the Act must be posted in a conspicuous position at the entry of the factory, and anywhere else the inspector may direct ; it should contain the name and address of the inspector and of the certifying surgeon, and state the clock (if any) by which times are fixed, the period of employment, meal times, and system on which children (if any) are employed. A notice stating the number of persons employed in each room, and notices of special regulations and exemptions (if any) under which a factory or workshop is worked must also be exhibited.

INSPECTION.—An inspector is authorised to inspect all parts of a factory or workshop; he may question any person employed, either in the presence of the employer or privately. He can also examine the various lists, registers⁶ and certificates which have to be kept in compliance with the Acts. Schools attended by children employed in factories and workshops are also open to inspection under these Acts.

NOTES.

(1.) The list of 19 classes of works which are included among non-textile factories, even when no power is used, will be found in the " Law relating to Factories and Workshops," p. 156. Seven other classes of works are defined as non-textile factories if power is used (*see ibid*, p. 158).

(2.) In addition to the factories mentioned in the text, factories where any process is carried on incident to the manufacture of flax, hemp, jute, tow, china grass, cocoa-nut fibre or other like material, are included under the definition of textile. This is the case whether the material is manufactured separately or together with other material. But print-works, bleaching and dyeing works, lace warehouses, paper-mills, flax scutch mills, rope works and hat works are specially exempted, and are considered as non-textile.

(3.) The legal hours of labour, as will appear in a later chapter, are not the same for domestic workshops, or for workshops from which children and young persons are excluded, as for ordinary workshops. The provisions of the Acts relating to meal times, affixing notices, holidays, accidents, and special rules for dangerous employments do not apply to domestic workshops.

(4.) Workshops, other than bakehouses, in which men only are employed, stand outside the Factory Acts for all matters but those dealt with under Sections 18, 20, and 21 of 1895 (*see* " Law relating to Factories and Workshops," pp. 196–7), they are treated as ordinary workshops for the purposes of the Public Health Acts.

(5.) The regulations for Scotland and Ireland are somewhat different (*see* " Law relating to Factories and Workshops," p. 106, note *b*).

(6.) For full details of registers and lists to be kept and notices to be sent to inspectors (*see* " Law relating to Factories and Workshops," p. 65).

CHAPTER II.

SANITATION.—The sanitary condition of workshops is, speaking generally, regulated by the Public Health Acts, that of factories by the Factory and Workshop Acts. For the purposes of the former the officers of the Sanitary Authority have the powers of factory inspectors, and the provisions of both Acts are very similar. If any legally remediable defect is not dealt with by the Sanitary Authority the factory inspector may give notice of the defect to the Sanitary Authority, and if no attention is paid to his notice he may, after a month has elapsed, take action himself.

Factories and workshops are required to be kept in a cleanly condition, and free from effluvia. Speaking generally, every factory has to be lime-washed once in 14 months, unless it is painted with oil or varnished every seven years, and also washed with hot soap and water every 14 months. In some other cases the regulations are more stringent, *e.g.*, where specially dirty or dangerous trades are carried on, and again others are exempt. No limit is prescribed by the Public Health Acts beyond which lime-washing may not be delayed in the workshop.[1]

In order to prevent over-crowding in factories and workshops a minimum space is required of 250 cubic feet for each person, and 400 cubic feet during overtime.[2]

A reasonable temperature must be maintained in all rooms in which work is carried on.[3]

A sufficient number of suitable sanitary conveniences must be provided for male and female workers separately.

Factories and workshops must be ventilated in such a way as to render harmless so far as is practicable all the gases, vapours, dust, and other impurities generated in the course of the work that may be injurious to health. An Inspector has power to insist on the use of mechanical means of ventilation, even in a workshop, if he thinks that inhalation of dust, gases, or other impurities by workers can be prevented by such means.

MACHINERY.—Certain parts of machinery considered as dangerous are required to be fenced, and such fencing must be kept in good repair. Children are forbidden to clean machinery in motion, and young persons dangerous machinery in motion. Women are allowed to clean any part of the machinery by which the work is actually done while in motion, but not the " mill-gearing," as it is called, by which power is transmitted from the first moving power to a machine.

There are further special regulations as to certain parts of the machinery, too technical for quotation here.

The use of dangerous premises may be prohibited under the Act. Alterations in dangerous machinery may be required or its use wholly forbidden.

FIRE.—The Sanitary Authority or County Council, or, in case of their failure to take action, a factory inspector, can require that certain precautions shall be taken in all factories and workshops, but these precautions differ for old and for new factories or workshops. Neither the main door nor the door of a room in which any person is at work may be fastened in such a way that it cannot be easily opened from the inside, and an Inspector has power in special cases to insist on movable fire escapes.

NOTES.

(1.) For further details as to cleanliness, *see* " Law relating to Factories and Workshops," p. 12.

If it seems to the Sanitary Authority that the health of the employés is suffering in any special workshop, orders may be given that the workshop or part of it shall be similarly cleansed, purified, or limewashed.—(" Law relating to Factories and Workshops," p. 14).

(2.) The minimum of cubic space per person required may be altered by the Home Secretary for the period of time during which artificial light (not including electric light) is used.

(3.) The Cotton Cloth Factories' Act, 1889, which regulates the moisture in the atmosphere in cotton factories, with any necessary modifications introduced by the Home Secretary, applies to all Textile Factories (not subject to special rules) in which artificial humidity is produced.

Ordinarily, the *occupier* is responsible for the sanitary condition of a factory, but in a tenement factory, *i.e.*, a factory parts of which are used for separate purposes, although supplied with mechanical power from the same source, the *owner* is responsible for these as well as for some other structural conditions.—(" Law relating to Factories and Workshops," p. 51).

CHAPTER III.

EMPLOYMENT.

(I.) HOURS OF WORK.—(1) ORDINARY EMPLOYMENT; (2) EXCEPTIONAL EMPLOYMENT.

(II.) MEAL TIMES.—(1) ORDINARY MEAL TIMES; (2) EXCEPTIONAL MEAL TIMES.

(III.) SPECIAL CONDITIONS OF EMPLOYMENT.— (1) EMPLOYMENT OF WOMEN AFTER CHILDBIRTH; (2) CERTIFICATES OF FITNESS; (3) STANDARD OF EDUCATION.

(IV.) HOLIDAYS. — (1) ORDINARY HOLIDAYS; (2) JEWISH HOLIDAYS.

(I.) HOURS OF WORK.

(1) Ordinary Employment.

(*a*) **WOMEN AND YOUNG PERSONS** may be employed in textile factories, non-textile factories, and workshops between 6 a.m. and 6 p.m. or 7 a.m. and 7 p.m. In non-textile factories and workshops the further alternative is allowed of working between 8 a.m. and 8 p.m.

On Saturdays the ordinary period in textile factories is between 6 a.m. and 12.30 p.m. or 7 a.m. and 1.30 p.m. for manufacturing purposes, with an extra half-hour for other purposes, *e.g.*, cleaning.

In non-textile factories and workshops the ordinary period on Saturdays is between 6 a.m. and 2 p.m., 7 a.m.

and 3 p.m., or 8 a.m. and 4 p.m.; or if a woman or young person has not been actually employed for more than eight hours on any day in the week, and notice of such non-employment has been duly affixed in the factory or workshop and served on the Inspector, she may be employed between 6 a.m. and 4 p.m, with an interval of not less than two hours for meals.

(*b*) **CHILDREN** may be employed in one of two ways—on alternate days in the week or in alternate sets on each day.

(1) **Alternate Sets.**—One set of children may begin at the same time as the young persons employed (*i.e.*, 6 a.m. or 7 a.m.) This set must end work at 1 p.m., or at the beginning of the dinner-hour if before 1 p.m. The afternoon set may begin at either of these times and end at the same time as the young persons. When the dinner-hour is not before 2 p.m. the afternoon set may begin at noon, provided the morning set stops work at noon.

A child may work on Saturday for the same number of hours as a young person, but he must not be employed for two Saturdays running. Further, if he has worked on any previous day in the week for more than five and a half hours he must not be employed at all on the Saturday.

A child must not be employed for two weeks running in the same set.

In non-textile factories and workshops the regulations are the same as in textile factories, with the following exceptions:—

In cases where young persons begin at 8 a.m. and end at 8 p.m., the morning set may begin at 8 a.m. and the afternoon set end at 8 p.m. The afternoon set may begin either at 1 p.m. or at the end of the dinner-hour if after 12.30 p.m.

On Saturday the afternoon set must leave off work at the same time as the young persons.

Children must be employed on Saturday in that set in which they have not been employed during the rest of the week. If during the first five days of the week they have been employed in a morning set, on the Saturday and for the first five days of the next week they must be employed in an afternoon set and *vice versâ.*

(2) **Alternate Days.**—This system is not in common use. The period of employment is the same as that for young persons, but a child must only be employed on alternate days, and must not be employed on the same days during two successive weeks.

The system is allowed as a substitute for alternate sets in factories and ordinary workshops but not in domestic workshops.

(c) **IN WOMEN'S WORKSHOPS,** that is in workshops from which young persons and children are excluded, women may be employed for a *specified* period of 12 hours between 6 a.m. and 10 p.m., and on Saturdays of 8 hours between 6 a.m. and 4 p.m.

These hours are only allowed when the employer has stated his intention on the prescribed abstract of conducting his workshop on this system.

(d) **IN DOMESTIC WORKSHOPS** women's hours are unrestricted.

The period of employment for young persons is between 6 a.m. and 9 p.m., less 4½ hours for meals and rest.

The regulations for the employment of children in alternate sets are similar to those in non-textile factories and workshops—6 a.m. to 1 p.m., or 1 p.m. to 8 p.m. ; Saturdays, 1 p.m. to 4 p.m.

(e) **EMPLOYMENT OUTSIDE A FACTORY OR WORKSHOP** in the business of the factory or workshop is prohibited (except during the authorised period) in the case of a child, on any day during which the child is employed in the factory or workshop, and in the case of a young person or woman, on any day in which the young person or woman is employed in the factory or workshop both before and after the dinner hour.

Taking home work is included as employment outside the factory or workshop.

Where the occupier of a factory or workshop also keeps a shop, he must not employ a young person or a woman in the factory or workshop, and in the shop, for a longer period than is allowed for his or her employment in the factory or workshop alone.   There is a similar provision in the Shop Hours Act, 1892, applying to young persons and children who are employed first in *any* factory or workshop, and then in a shop, to the knowledge of the shopkeeper.

(2) Exceptional Employment.

(a) IN TEXTILE FACTORIES overtime may not be worked by women, young persons or children.

In *warehouses attached to textile factories, i.e.,* places in which persons are solely employed in polishing, cleaning, wrapping and packing up goods, it may be worked by women but not by young persons or children.

In a textile, as well as in a non-textile factory, driven by water-power alone and liable to be stopped by drought or flood, overtime is permitted under certain conditions for women and young persons. This is the only exception to the prohibition of overtime for protected persons in textile factories and it is very seldom claimed.

(b) IN CERTAIN NON-TEXTILE FACTORIES AND WORKSHOPS overtime is permitted.

It is permitted for children on one plea only—that is when the process is in an incomplete state. A list of the factories to which this exception applies will be found at the end of the chapter.[1]

Young persons may work overtime in those factories. They may also work overtime in the following cases—

(1) When damage may arise from spontaneous combustion in Turkey red dyeing, or from extraordinary atmospheric influences in open-air bleaching.

(2) In factories where water-power alone is used and stoppage may be feared from drought or flood.

These are the only three grounds upon which overtime for young persons is permitted.

C

Women may work overtime in all the cases mentioned above in which it is permitted for children and young persons, and in the following places as well—

(1) Warehouses (whether attached to textile or to non-textile factories or workshops).

(2) Non-textile factories or workshops where a sudden press of business is common.

(3) Non-textile factories or workshops where goods of a perishable nature are dealt with.

A reference for the list of trades to which these exemptions have been granted will be found at the end of the chapter, and the conditions under which overtime is permitted are given below.

(c) **CONDITIONS OF OVERTIME WHEN PERMITTED.**

(1) **Factories Liable to Stoppage by Drought or Flood.** — (Women and Young Persons.) — Employment is authorised from 6 a.m. to 9 p.m.

This overtime must not be worked, when the damage is from drought, on more than 96 days, or, from flood, on more than 48 days, in the year. It must not extend beyond the time already lost during the previous twelve months.

(2) **When the Process is in an Incomplete State.**—(Women, Young Persons, and Children.)— Employment is authorised for an extra half-hour at the end of the day's work in order to complete an incomplete process.

Such extra half-hours must be deducted from the total period for the week.

(3) **Turkey Red Dyeing and Open Air Bleaching.**—(Women and Young Persons.)—Employment is authorised " so far as is necessary " to prevent damage from the causes stated above.

Forms must be exhibited in all cases where these exemptions are claimed, otherwise the overtime is not legal. They are not given in detail, as it is improbable that such cases would come under the notice of those for whom this book is intended.

(4) **Warehouses and Non-Textile Factories and Workshops where a Sudden Press of Business is Common.**[2]—(Women only.)—Overtime is authorised, but may not be worked—

> For more than 2 hours in any day.
> For more than 3 days in any week.
> For more than 30 days in any year.

Out of the extra period of two hours one half-hour must be allowed for meals, and it must be after 5 p.m.

The following conditions as to notices must be observed. These must be affixed in the factory or workshop :—

(1) A notice showing that leave has been obtained from the Home Office to work overtime.

(2) A notice (known as the Overtime Record), containing spaces for the entry of each of the 30 days' overtime.

Each entry must be made *before the overtime is begun.* Thus, if the ordinary period is 8 to 8, the overtime must be entered before 8 p.m. on the day on which it is intended to work it.

The date of the month, and the hour set apart for the extra meal hour, must also be entered on the form at the same time.

(3) Entry must be made of the date and intended duration of the overtime *before it is begun* in the Overtime Register, and notice must be sent to the Home Office from this register also before the overtime is begun.

(5) Where Perishable Articles are Dealt with overtime is authorised (women only), but it may not be worked—

For more than 2 hours in any day.
For more than 5 days in any week.
For more than 60 days in any year.
No work may be carried on after 9 p.m.

The conditions as to notices are the same as under (4), but the Record contains 60 spaces.

(d) PLACES IN WHICH THE ORDINARY PERIOD OF EMPLOYMENT MAY BE ALTERED.

The period of employment may in certain cases be 9 a.m. to 9 p.m. for young persons and women if a special order to that effect be obtained from the Home Secretary. But if children are employed, the afternoon set must stop work at 8 p.m.

Such an order has been granted in the following cases.—

(1) Workshops in which the curing of fish is carried on.

(2) Factories in the metropolis in which book-binding is carried on from September to February inclusive.

(3) Workshops in connection with drapers' retail establishments in the boroughs of Manchester and Salford.

(4) Factories and workshops for the manufacture of straw hats and bonnets.

In the last three cases the minimum space of 400 cubic feet—usually required only during overtime—must be allowed.

In straw hat and bonnet factories, as a condition of the exemption, no young person or woman can, under any circumstances, be employed after 9 p.m.

In Turkey red dyeing women and young persons may be employed till 4.30 p.m. on Saturdays if the additional hours have been deducted on previous days.[3]

(e) EMPLOYMENT IN JEWISH WORK-SHOPS.—If a Jewish occupier keeps his premises closed on Saturdays till sunset he may employ young persons and women after that time until 9 p.m.

If he keeps his premises closed during the whole of Saturday he may employ young persons and women

for an additional hour during the first five days of the
week. This additional hour must not be before 6 a.m.
nor after 9 p.m.

He may employ such of his workpeople as are Jews
by religion on Sundays, provided that his premises are
closed during the whole of Saturday.   In this case either
Sunday or Friday must be treated as Saturday as regards
a shorter period of employment.

The factory or workshop must not be open for
traffic on Sundays.

(II.) MEAL TIMES.

(1) Ordinary.

(*a*) **TEXTILE FACTORIES.**—Two hours must be
allowed for meals to women and young persons during
the period of employment.

No women, young persons, or children may be
employed for more than 4½ hours without an interval of
at least half-an hour for a meal.[4]

All women, young persons and children must have
meals at the same time, and must not stay during meal
times in a room where work is being carried on.

On Saturdays at least half-an-hour must be allowed
for meals. If the period of employment is from 6 a.m.
to 1.30 p.m., one hour must be allowed.

(*b*) **NON-TEXTILE FACTORIES AND WORK-
SHOPS.**— One and a-half hours must be allowed for
meals during the period of employment.

No woman, young person, or child may be employed for more than five hours without an interval of at least half-an-hour for a meal.

Meals must be simultaneous, and no woman, young person, or child must stay during meal times in a room where work is being carried on.

On Saturdays at least half-an-hour must be allowed for meals. If the period of employment is 6 a.m. to 4 p.m. two hours must be allowed.

(c) DOMESTIC AND WOMEN'S WORKSHOPS.

There are no provisions as to fixed meal times applying to domestic workshops. Young persons must be allowed $4\frac{1}{2}$ hours for meals and absence from work out of the 6 a.m. to 9 p.m. period.

In women's workshops, *i.e.*, workshops conducted on the system of excluding young persons and children, a specified period of one and a-half hours on ordinary days, and half-an-hour on Saturdays, must be allowed for meals.

(2) Exceptional.

(a) In certain trades, the number of which the Home Secretary has power to extend, meal times need not be simultaneous.[5]

(b) Exemptions may also be made from the regulation prohibiting protected persons from remaining during meal times in a room where work is being carried on.

In both these cases a notice must be affixed, stating that such an exemption has been obtained.

(c) In certain parts of some factories and workshops, women, young persons and children are not allowed to remain during meal times even when no work is being carried on.[6]

(III.) SPECIAL CONDITIONS OF EMPLOYMENT.

(1) **EMPLOYMENT OF WOMEN AFTER CHILD-BIRTH.**—Women may not be employed in factories or workshops within four weeks after child-birth.

(2) **CERTIFICATES OF FITNESS.**— Young persons under 16 and children working in factories are required to have certificates of fitness for employment.

These certificates are obtained from the certifying surgeon and must state (1) the age of the young person or child, (2) that he or she is not unfitted by bodily infirmity for employment in that factory.

In the case of any special child working in either a factory or workshop who appears unfit for employment, an inspector may require that he shall be discharged within a given time unless a certificate (in the former case a renewed certificate) can be obtained from the certifying surgeon.

Certificates of fitness are under no circumstances required in laundries.

(3) **STANDARD OF EDUCATION.**—Children may not be employed (except out of school hours) unless they have reached the standard of education fixed locally for exemption from full school attendance.

Children between 13 and 14 may leave school altogether and be employed as young persons if they have gained the necessary certificates.

Details as to the standard of proficiency required in England and Wales are given on p. 22.

(IV.) HOLIDAYS.

(1) ORDINARY HOLIDAYS.—No women, young persons and children are allowed to work on Sundays in factories or workshops (except where night work is allowed for male young persons,[3] and, as above given, for Jews in Jewish workshops and factories, p. 38).

On Saturdays, as has been stated already, the period of employment must be less than on other days.

In certain non-textile factories and workshops a weekly short day may be substituted for Saturday, but a notice must be exhibited in the factory or workshop showing that leave has been obtained.[7]

Six holidays must be allowed during the year to all women, young persons, and children employed in factories and workshops, other than domestic workshops.

In England and Wales the fixed holidays are Christmas Day, Good Friday, and the four Bank Holidays.

For any of these, including probably Christmas Day, an employer may, by giving due notice, substitute either another whole holiday or two half holidays.

Reference for details as to the holidays fixed for Scotland and Ireland are given at the end of the chapter.[8]

If an occupier wishes to substitute other whole or half-holidays for the fixed days, he must affix a notice stating the proposed holidays during the first week of January, and must send a notice to the inspector. He may make a further change later in the year by giving fourteen days' notice in a similar way.

At least half of the holidays allowed during the year must fall between March 15th and October 1st.

(2) JEWISH HOLIDAYS.—As already explained above, a Jewish occupier may employ such of his work-people as are Jews by religion on Sundays provided that his premises are closed during the whole of Saturday. But in this case either Sunday or Friday must be treated as Saturday as regards a shorter period of employment.

A Jewish occupier may, if all the women, young persons, and children whom he employs are of his own religion, substitute two bank holidays for Christmas Day and Good Friday, but must not keep his factory or work-shop open for traffic on Christmas Day or Good Friday.

The provisions respecting notice of holidays other than the fixed holidays apply to Jewish occupiers also.

NOTES.

(1.) Women, young persons, and *children* are allowed to work an extra half-hour to complete a process (under the conditions already stated) in the following places :—

(*a*.) Bleaching and dyeing works.

(*b*.) Print works.

(*c*.) Iron mills in which male young persons are not employed during any part of the night.

(*d.*) Foundries in which male young persons are not employed during any part of the night.

(*e.*) Paper mills in which male young persons are not employed during any part of the night.

(2.) For the lists of trades in which overtime is allowed because the materials are liable to be spoilt by weather, because there may be a sudden press of work, or the goods are regarded as perishable, *see* "Law relating to Factories and Workshops," pp. 153-155.

(3.) For alterations of hours permitted in the case of male young persons only, *see* "Law relating to Factories and Workshops," page 26.

(4.) For exceptions to the 4½ hours spell in certain textile factories, *see* "Law relating to Factories and Workshops," pages 118-156.

(5.) For exceptions to the regulations as to meals for children, young persons, and women being simultaneous, and as to their not remaining in a room where work is being carried on, *see* "Law relating to Factories and Workshops," pp. 151-152.

(6.) For the places in which protected persons are forbidden to remain during meal hours, whether work is being carried on or not, *see* "Law relating to Factories and Workshops," p. 150.

(7.) For the cases in which another half-holiday may be substituted for Saturday, *see* "Law relating to Factories and Workshops," p. 117.

(8.) For Scotch and Irish holidays, *see* "Law relating to Factories and Workshops," pp. 39 and 40.

Chapter IV.

LAUNDRIES AND BAKEHOUSES.

LAUNDRIES.—Until 1895 laundries did not come within the scope of the Factory and Workshop Acts, but were subject to the Public Health Acts only. In 1895 some of the provisions of the Acts were extended to them, but they cannot be regarded as on the same footing as factories or workshops. For this reason it is clearer to explain their position in a separate chapter.

Only those laundries in which trade is carried on for the sake of profit are taken account of in the Acts. Laundries connected with private houses or institutions where washing is done not as a trade or for purpose of gain are not included. For instance, a laundry attached to Turkish baths would not come under the Acts.

There are, further, three classes of laundries which are exempted :—

(*a.*) Laundries where all the workers are inmates of a prison, industrial school, or similar institution whose inspection is otherwise provided for.

(*b.*) Laundries where all the workers are inmates of a religious or charitable institution.

(*c.*) Laundries in which members of the same family and not more than two other persons are employed.

Children may be employed in a laundry for 10 hours in one day, provided that the total number of hours in the week does not exceed 30; young persons for 12 hours in one day, and 60 per week; women for 14 hours in one day, and 60 per week. No overtime is allowed for young persons and children. Women are on no account allowed to work more than fourteen hours in the day. Provided that this limit is not exceeded, they may work two hours overtime on 30 days in the year. Overtime must not be worked on more than three days in the same week. It must be observed that these regulations for hours do not entail a regular legal working day. The number of hours may vary on each day in the week, and the period of employment may begin or end at any hour of the day or night. Lists, indeed, must be posted, stating the period of employment and meal times, but these may be varied each day before the work begins. The only regulation with regard to meal times is that no women, children, or young persons may be employed for more than 5 hours continuously without being allowed at least half-an-hour for a meal.

The provision requiring an extra half-hour's interval for this purpose after 5 p.m. during overtime has not been extended to laundries.

The following special sanitary regulations are enforced in laundries where mechanical power is used :—

(a.) A fan or other means of a proper construction shall be provided, maintained, and used for regulating the temperature in every ironing-room, and for carrying away the steam in every washhouse in the laundry ; and (*b.*) All stoves for heating irons shall be sufficiently separated from any ironing-room, and gas irons emitting any noxious fumes shall not be used ; and

(*c.*) The floors shall be kept in good condition and drained in such manner as will allow the water to flow off freely.

The occupier of a laundry or contractor who gives out washing to be done in a building where anyone is ill with scarlet fever or small-pox is liable to a fine.

Children and young persons working in a laundry do not require to be medically certified as fit for employment.

The provisions of the Acts respecting matters not specially mentioned in this chapter—sanitary provisions, safety, accidents, &c.—apply to laundries as though they were either factories or workshops. Laundries in which mechanical power is used are, for these purposes, regarded as factories; those in which power is not used as workshops.[1]

BAKEHOUSES are regarded by the law as non-textile factories if mechanical power is used, and otherwise as workshops. They are defined as "places in which are baked bread, biscuits, or confectionery, from the baking of which a profit is derived."

Several special additional regulations apply to them. No place *underground* may be used for a bakehouse unless so used before 1895.

The regulations as to sanitation and cleanliness are

particularly stringent. Details are given at the end of the chapter.[2]

A room in the same building and on the same floor as a bakehouse must not be used as a sleeping room unless it is entirely separated from the bakehouse by a partition reaching from the floor to the ceiling. Further, such a room must be provided with an external window of not less than 9 sq. feet, of which 4½ sq. feet are made to open.

In the case of an insanitary bakehouse the Court has power, instead of or in addition to fining the occupier in the ordinary way, to order him to remove the cause of complaint, a penalty of £1 being imposed for every day of delay.

The Sanitary Authority has power to enforce the special sanitary provisions in workshop bakehouses. The other provisions are administered by the factory inspectors, as are all provisions in factory bakehouses.[3]

NOTES.

(1.) For the special requirements relating to laundries, *see* " Law relating to Factories and Workshops," p. 198.

(2.) No water-closet, earth-closet, privy or ashpit may be within, or in direct communication with, the bakehouse. A cistern supplying water to a bakehouse must be quite separate from that supplying water to a water-closet. No drain or pipe for carrying off fæcal or sewage matter may have an opening within the bakehouse.

(3.) The inside of every bakehouse must be completely painted with oil, varnished or lime-washed, or part of it must be painted or varnished and the remainder lime-washed. There must be three coats of the paint or varnish, renewed every seven years, and washed with hot water and soap every six months. The lime-washing must be renewed every six months.

Bakehouses are exempted from the provisions of the general law in the following particulars :—

(1.) Male young persons over 16 may be employed between 5 a.m. and 9 p.m. under certain conditions.

(2.) Women are allowed to work overtime in biscuit-baking.

(3.) Children, young persons, and women may work an extra half-hour at the end of the day.

(4.) The regulations providing that meal-times shall be simultaneous, and that protected persons shall not be allowed to remain in a room where work is carried on during meal-times, do not apply to factory bakehouses in which travelling ovens are used.

CHAPTER V.

OUTWORKERS.

LISTS OF OUTWORKERS.—In certain trades occupiers, and contractors employed by them, are required to keep lists of all whom they employ outside the factory or workshop whether as workers or contractors.[1]

These lists, which must be sent to the inspector for the district twice in the year, are useful in supplying the inspectors with the addresses of domestic and other small workshops which might otherwise escape inspection altogether. They are also a useful aid to detection in cases where work is illegally given out to workers who have been employed in a factory or workshop during the day (both before and after the dinner-hour).

EMPLOYMENT INSIDE AND OUTSIDE A FACTORY OR WORKSHOP on the same day.

The following provisions of the Factory Acts relate to this matter :—

A young person or woman shall not, except during the period of employment, be employed in the business of a factory or workshop outside the factory or workshop on any day during which the young person or woman is employed in the factory or workshop both before and after the dinner hour.

A child shall not, except during the period of employment, be employed in the business of a factory or workshop on any day during which the child is employed in the factory or workshop (p. 32).

EMPLOYMENT IN A FACTORY OR WORKSHOP AND IN A SHOP on the same day.

If a young person or woman[2] is employed by the same employer on the same day both in a factory or workshop and in a shop, the whole period of employment of that young person or woman shall not exceed the number of hours permitted by the Factory Acts for his or her employment in the factory or workshop (p. 32).

GIVING OUT OF WORK.—In addition to the regulations applying to domestic and other workshops, which have been explained elsewhere (Chapter III.), the following special provision applies to places in which wearing apparel is made, cleaned or repaired. The occupier of a factory, workshop, laundry, or other place from which such work is given out, or any contractor employed by him, is liable to a fine if he allows work to be given out to be done in any house where a person is ill of scarlet fever or small-pox.

There is, further, a provision intended to prevent the employment of outworkers in unhealthy places. Unfortunately, however, the section is so worded that the condition of such a place would have to be injurious not only to the health of persons employed there but also to that of the whole neighbourhood. The section has never been brought into force, and could not, it is held, be enforced except in the case of an epidemic.

NOTES.

(1.) The trades in which lists of outworkers must be kept are the manufacture of articles of wearing apparel and of electro-plate, cabinet and furniture-making, upholstery, file-making, and fur-pulling. In the case of wearing apparel, any place from which it is given out is regarded as a workshop.

(2.) For cases in which the employment of a child is regulated, see *infra*, Chap. VII., p. 61.

CHAPTER VI.

PARTICULARS OF WAGES AND TRUCK ACTS.

The Factory and Workshop Acts do not regulate the *amount* paid in wages. But both the Truck Acts and what is known as the " Particulars Clause " (sec. 40 Factory and Workshop Act, 1895), are intended to ensure that the wages agreed upon by employer and employed are really paid.

THE PARTICULARS CLAUSE.—It is provided in the textile trades that the worker shall know beforehand particulars of the work to be done and the amount to be received for it. The payment of this amount can be enforced by law. The particulars of a piece of work to be done must in all the textile trades be given to an employé in writing unless ascertainable by an automatic indicator. An employer who tampers with or uses a false indicator is liable to a fine. If a worker tampers with an indicator he also is liable to a fine.

In the worsted and woollen weaving trades (with the exception of hosiery) the particulars of wages must be supplied separately in writing to each worker, and also shown on a placard in a conspicuous position. In the other textile trades they are generally furnished separately in writing only. But if the same particulars are applicable to all the workers in one room a placard may be used instead. Any worker who uses this knowledge of particulars in order to disclose a trade secret, or any person who induces him or her to do so, is liable to a fine.

The Home Secretary may, if he think it desirable, extend the provisions of the Particulars Clause with any necessary modifications to any class of non-textile factories or workshops. Such an order has been made in the case of places in which handkerchiefs, aprons, pinafores, blouses, chains and anchors, locks, latches, keys, and felt hats are made, and wholesale tailoring is done.

THE TRUCK ACTS.[1]—These Acts are applied to laundries and places to which work is given out from factories and workshops as well as to factories and workshops.

The main object of the earlier Truck Acts was to prevent an employer from giving a worker[2] goods as wages instead of coin of the realm. I propose to deal with this part of the subject before passing to the consideration of the Truck Act of 1896, which was designed to control excessive fines and deductions for materials, &c.

It is illegal for an employer to pay his workers their wages in goods or to give them tickets to be exchanged for goods instead of coin of the realm. It is also illegal for him to insist on their wages being spent in a certain way. There is, however, nothing to prevent a worker from making purchases at his employer's shop; but in that case, if he refuse to pay the employer could not recover.   Such purchases would, therefore, be made with ready money.

The employer may, *if a written agreement is made* with an employé, whose signature it must bear, supply him or her with medicine, medical attendance, fuel, or victuals cooked and eaten under the employer's roof,[3] and he may let to him the whole or any part of a tenement ;   or, if a miner, he may supply him with materials, tools or implements needed for his work, or hay, corn, or other provender for his horses or other beasts used in the course of his employment.   For these goods or materials, the medicine or medical attendance so supplied, or for money advanced in respect of them, or for the rent, the employer may make a deduction, but it must not exceed the " real and true value" of the fuel, materials, tools, hay, corn, and provender.

An employer may advance money to a worker in illness, for contribution to a Friendly Society, or Savings Bank, or for his children's education, and deduct the sum advanced from wages without a separate agreement.

Deductions for sharpening or repairing tools require a separate agreement, but this need not necessarily be in writing.

Contracts obliging a worker to expend part of his or her wages in contributions to benefit, pension societies, &c., are not considered as on the same footing as contracts for the purchase of goods.   Such contracts are therefore not illegal, but an employer must, once a year, submit the accounts to be audited on behalf of the workers.

It is not illegal for an employé to authorise his employer to pay his or her wages to some other person.

THE TRUCK ACT OF 1896 regulates the amount
which may be deducted by an employer for (*a*) fines,
(*b*) deductions for spoilt goods, (*c*) deductions for
materials, &c.

Sums paid or deducted contrary to this Act may be
recovered by the worker or shop assistant, if the action is
brought within six months; but if he has acquiesced in
the deduction or payment he can only recover the excess
(if any) over the amount which the Court finds it would
have been fair and reasonable to demand.

FINES are only allowed in cases where an act or
omission causes, or might cause, some damage to the
employer. They may only be inflicted if the terms of
the contract are posted in a conspicuous position, or if
the contract is in writing and signed by the employé.

The contract must contain details of all fines which
it is proposed to inflict, and on each occasion on which a
fine is inflicted the employé must be told in writing why
it is inflicted and the amount.

No fines must be imposed, or notice posted of possible fines, which are not fair and reasonable.[4] A register
of fines inflicted, with particulars as to the reason of
infliction, must be kept by the employer and produced
by him when required by the inspector.

A copy of the notice of fines must be given either to
an inspector or an employé who demands it.

These sections only, relating to fines, apply to shop
assistants, but their enforcement is not part of the duty
either of factory inspectors or inspectors under the
Shop Hours Act.

DEDUCTIONS FOR BAD OR NEGLIGENT WORK or injury to the property of the employer. The terms of the contract under which an employer may deduct for bad work must, like that for fines, be exhibited in a conspicuous position, or the contract must be in writing, signed by the worker, and he or she must be supplied with particulars in writing each time a deduction is made. A copy must also be supplied to the worker or to an inspector, if demanded, and a register must be kept. Such deductions must not exceed in amount the actual or estimated damage or loss sustained by the employer, and must be " fair and reasonable," all the circumstances of the case being taken into consideration. A deduction, under these conditions, may be made from the wages of the person who either caused the damage, or had control over, or had by contract agreed to be responsible for the person at fault.

DEDUCTIONS FOR MATERIALS, tools, machines, standing room, light, heat, or anything else supplied to the worker by the employer in relation to his work must not in the case of materials or tools exceed the actual or estimated cost[5] to the employer, or in the other cases a fair and reasonable charge.[6]

The conditions as to posting up the terms of the contract, &c., are the same as in the case of deductions for bad work.

NOTES.

(1.) The Home Secretary has power to exempt any class of persons from the provisions of the Truck Act, 1896, if he think it advisable. The cotton weavers of Lancashire, Cheshire, Derbyshire, and the West Riding have been so exempted.

(2.) The definition of workman, by which the Acts are governed, is that of the Employers' and Workmen's Act, which is explained in the chapter on Compensation for Accidents, page 64. A person who manufactures for sale articles of less than £5 in value is considered as employed by the shopkeeper or dealer to whom he sells them.

(3.) Servants in husbandry did not come within the scope of the first Truck Act, 1831, and the Truck Act, 1887, contains a special clause allowing employers to supply them by contract with food, non-alcoholic drink, cottages, &c., in addition to wages in coin.

(4.) It may be observed that, since only fair and reasonable lists of fines and deductions may be posted, and in the cases of fines the amount must be mentioned, in the former cases action can be taken on a list which is not fair and reasonable even though no fine has actually been inflicted.

(5.) The words "actual or estimated" as applied to the amount of loss sustained by an employer through bad work, or the cost or materials or tools supplied by him, are intended to insure that no profit shall in either case accrue to the employer. "Estimated" may be held to permit a margin for cost or storage, or superintendence, but an employer ought in no case to sell such goods at retail prices, since retail prices allow for profit on the goods sold.

(6.) The Hosiery Manufacture (Wages) Act and the Coal Mines Regulation Act contain special provisions with regard to deductions for persons employed in those trades.

Chapter VII.

EMPLOYMENT IN SHOPS.

HOURS.—The employment of young persons in shops is controlled by the Shop Hours Acts, 1892—1895, but that of women is unrestricted. Under these Acts " young persons " means *anyone* under the age of 18 ; the definition, therefore, covers *children.*[1]

A young person may not be employed in or about a shop for more than 74 hours in the week, including meal times.

Further, if a young person has, on the same day, to the knowledge of the employer, been already employed in *any* factory or workshop, the total number of hours during which he or she is employed must not exceed the hours permitted by the Factory and Workshop Acts.

Although the employment of women is not regulated by the Shop Hours Acts, it is indirectly regulated by the Factory and Workshop Acts where a woman is employed on the same day in a shop and in a factory or workshop kept by the same person.[2]

NOTICE.—A notice referring to the provisions of the Acts, and stating how long a young person may be employed, must be posted in all shops where young persons are employed.

INSPECTION.—Inspectors under the Acts may be appointed by a County or Borough Council. Their powers are like those of inspectors under the Factory and Workshop Acts.

EXEMPTED PERSONS.—The provisions of the Acts do not apply to members of the same family living in a house of which the shop forms part, or to members of the employer's family so living, or to any one wholly employed as a domestic servant.

FINES.—As has been explained in the chapter on " Particulars of Wages and Truck Acts," the provisions respecting fines apply to shop assistants, but it is not the duty of an inspector under the Shop Hours Acts to see that they are enforced.

NOTES.

(1.) " Shop " means retail and wholesale shops, markets, stalls and warehouses in which assistants are employed for hire, and includes licensed public-houses and refreshment houses of any kind.

(2.) See *supra*, p. 32.

CHAPTER VIII.

COMPENSATION FOR ACCIDENTS.

It is impossible in a single chapter to give more than a mere outline of so complicated a subject as that of an employer's liability to pay compensation to his workers for accidents suffered by them. Our readers will find in the Preface practical advice as to the best way of helping any cases they may come across.

An employer is in some measure responsible for the safety of those employed by him. But various methods of procedure may be open to an injured workman or his dependents :—

(*a*) Employer's liability at Common Law.

- (*b*) Employers' Liability Act, 1880.

(*c*) Workmen's Compensation Act, 1897.

(*a*) **EMPLOYER'S LIABILITY AT COMMON LAW.**—A master is bound to consider the safety of any of his servants, but his liability is subject to the following limitations :—

> (1.) If the accident was caused by the negligence of a fellow-servant of the injured man (even if it be that of a responsible foreman or manager) the master is not held liable, unless he can be shown to have been personally negligent in employing an

incompetent person.   This is known as the *Doctrine of Common Employment.*

(2.) If a servant knowingly exposes himself to danger in the course of his work he is supposed to have willingly accepted the risk.   This is known as *Volenti non fit injuria.*

(3.) If a worker's own negligence is the direct cause of the accident, a master, even though personally negligent, is held altogether free from blame. This is known as the *Doctrine of Contributory Negligence.*   To state the matter briefly:—An action will not lie against a master at Common Law unless it can be shown that he was *personally* negligent, and that the injured man's (or woman's) own negligence was not the cause or partial cause of the accident.[1]

(*b*) EMPLOYERS' LIABILITY ACT, 1880.— This Act does not apply to servants generally, but only to railway servants and workmen as defined in the Employers' and Workmen's Act of 1875.   Domestic and menial servants, and, under certain conditions, apprentices, are excluded by this definition.   The test in doubtful cases would be whether manual labour formed a substantial or merely incidental part of employment.

By the Act of 1880 the doctrine of common employment was modified, and the master became liable under it in various cases for which he had hitherto escaped liability.   Details of these differences will be found in the notes at the end of the chapter.[2]

Contributory negligence is a bar to action precisely as at Common Law.

It is possible to " contract out " of this Act—that is, the worker may sign an agreement which debars him from bringing an action under the Employers' Liability Act while in the service of that employer. Such an agreement may or may not be a condition of hiring.

Notice of an accident must be sent in to the employer within six weeks after its occurrence, and an action must be brought within six months, or, in case of death, within a year from the time when the accident happened. A specimen Form of Notice will be found in the notes at the end of the chapter.[3]

(c) WORKMEN'S COMPENSATION ACT, 1897.

—This Act came into force July 1st, 1898. Its application is limited to employment in factories and in certain specified trades, mentioned below.[4]

For the purpose of this Act the question involved is no longer one of negligence on the part of the employer or any of his servants. The Act is based on an entirely different principle. It is regarded as part of the contract between employer and employed that the latter shall be compensated for all accidents "arising out of and in the course of" his or her employment. The exceptions are in cases where the accident does not disable the workman for a period of at least two weeks from earning full wages, or where the accident was caused by the " serious and wilful misconduct " of the worker injured, and the onus of proving this lies on the employer.

It is provided that when work is done under a sub-contractor and an accident occurs, the principal contractor is liable to pay compensation in accordance with

E

the Act to the injured workman, but he can recover the amount he pays from the sub-contractor.

The Workmen's Compensation Act is limited in application to those employed in or about railways, factories, mines, quarries, engineering works, and buildings over 30 feet in height, which are being built, repaired, or pulled down (provided that scaffolding or mechanical power is in use). Although the Act is confined to these trades the interpretation of " workmen " is wider than that of the Employers' Liability Act. The Act applies to any person (either man or woman) working at one of the included trades, whether employed in manual labour or not. For instance, a clerk in a factory would be on the same footing as the other employés.

NOTICE OF ACCIDENT.—A written notice, like that given in the notes, should be sent in to the employer, giving the name and address of the person injured, with the date and cause of the accident.

This notice should state whether the accident has been fatal or not. It must be sent as soon as possible after the accident by or in behalf of the injured person. Although no definite limit of time is given in the Workmen's Compensation Act, except that in any case it must be sent before the workman has voluntarily left the employment in which he was injured, it is advisable that notice should be sent within six weeks after the occurrence of the accident. This is the limit under the Employers' Liability Act, and it might subsequently seem desirable to take action under that Act. It should be posted in a registered letter, or sent by a trustworthy messenger. Even if the foreman or some other person undertakes to report the accident, or the employer voluntarily promises compensation, it is safer to send such a notice.

CLAIM FOR COMPENSATION.—Compensation should be claimed from the employer within six months of the accident, or, in case of death, six months from the time of death.

ARBITRATION.—A fundamental difference between the Act of 1897 and that of 1880, or the procedure at Common Law is that under the former the matter is to be settled by arbitration, unless it has been already arranged by a voluntary agreement between employer and employed. The arbitrators to whom the matter is referred may be a committee representing employer and employed or any single person chosen by them. If such a committee is already in existence the matter must be brought before it for arbitration or further reference, unless a written objection is sent by one of the parties to the other before the committee meets to consider the matter. If the parties cannot agree on the committee or a single arbitrator, the County Court Judge will act as arbitrator, or may appoint a substitute. Where it is necessary to appoint a new arbitrator, a Judge of the High Court at Chambers may make the appointment on the application of either party.[5]

Arbitrators have power to settle the amount to be paid as compensation within the limits prescribed by the Act. No compensation can be exacted for the first fortnight after the accident.

A memorandum of the award must be sent by the

arbitrator to the registrar of the County Court, and can then be enforced as a County Court judgment.

Costs of the arbitration (other than the payment of an arbitrator appointed by the County Court Judge, which payment is specially provided for) are at the discretion of the arbitrators, except that they shall not exceed the limit prescribed by rules of court.

If an employer has already paid any sum to the worker in virtue of his accident, such a sum must be taken into consideration by the arbitrators in settling the amount to be paid as compensation. The same holds good in cases where the employer is guilty of a breach of the law relating to factories, workshops or mines, and the fine or part of the fine inflicted has been devoted to the benefit of the injured person.

AMOUNT OF COMPENSATION.—The amounts of compensation which can be received under the Act of 1897 are as follows :—

If the injured man dies leaving dependents* who were supported entirely by him, they may receive a sum equivalent to his earnings for three years or £150, whichever is the larger. (If he or she has been employed for less than three years the sum will be 156 times his or her average weekly wage during the actual period of employment.) In no case must they receive less than £150 or more than £300. The arbitrators may order this sum to be invested or otherwise used for the benefit of dependents.

If the dependents had other means of support they will receive a sum in no case greater than this, the exact amount being left to the discretion of the arbitrators.

If there are no dependents a sum not exceeding £10 can be obtained for funeral and medical expenses.

In the case of partial or total disablement the sum received must not exceed 50 per cent. of the average weekly earnings, or £1 per week.

The employer can commute the weekly payment at the end of six months by a lump sum, to be fixed by the arbitrators.

In settling the amount of this weekly payment at lump sum the arbitrators must take into consideration the difference between what a worker was able to earn before and would be able to earn after the accident. Any money paid by the employer in virtue of the accident must also be considered.

A weekly payment or sum down cannot be given away, charged—*i.e.*, pledged or gaged as security for debt—or attached—*i.e.*, taken by a creditor—or set off against a debt of the worker to the employer, and is inalienable by, say, bankruptcy.

If the injured man should die after the receipt of weekly payments the sum so expended would be deducted from the amount paid as compensation to his dependents.

At Common Law there is no limit to the sum which may be paid as compensation.

Under the Act of 1880 the limit is the estimated earnings of the injured man during three years. The Compensation Act allows no compensation for the first fortnight after the accident, and nothing is paid (except in the case of death without dependents) for medical or other expenses, or as a solatium.

It is usually possible, therefore, in not very serious accidents to obtain more by proceeding at Common Law or under the Act of 1880, if the case can be brought under them, than by the Workmen's Compensation Act, but it must be remembered that Court fees are not payable in the latter case and the costs are likely to be less.

ALTERNATIVE PROCEEDINGS.—It is possible to bring an action at Common Law, or under the Employers' Liability Act, and yet retain a right to compensation under the Workmen's Compensation Act should such an action fail. But the employer cannot be made to compensate again where a previous action has been successful. In order to deter workmen from unnecessary litigation the judge has power, where a previous action has been unsuccessful, to deduct the extra costs incurred through it from the sum obtained as compensation.

MEDICAL ATTENDANCE.—The injured person is obliged to submit to medical examination at the employer's expense if required to do so. A refusal would nullify his claim under this Act. In cases where the arbitrator has settled that a sum shall be paid weekly as compensation by the employer, contractor or any other person, the person making such payment can demand that the worker shall at any time see a doctor chosen by him. Doctors appointed by the Home Secretary and paid by the State may be called in by the arbitrators at any stage in the proceedings, and in the case of a weekly payment the workman may appeal to them from the decision of the doctor employed by the person who was making compensation.

CONTRACTING OUT.—"Contracting out" of the Workmen's Compensation Act is only allowed in favour of schemes which have been certified by the Registrar-General of Friendly Societies. Such a certificate is intended to secure that the scheme substituted by the employer is " on the whole not less favourable " to the workman than the Act itself. In cases where a certificate has been granted the workman may appeal to the registrar to re-consider the matter, and he has power, if desirable, to revoke the certificate. No such certified scheme can contain a clause obliging the worker to join the scheme as a condition of hiring.

NOTES.

(1.) In the case of death caused by an accident the dependents have no remedy at Common Law except under Lord Campbell's Act. This Act is entitled " An Act for Compensating the Families of Persons killed by Accidents."

(2.) The cases in which the Employers' Liability Act sets aside the doctrine of common employment are as follows:—a master is held liable when an accident happens through a defect in the " ways, works, machinery or plant," if such a defect is due to his own negligence, or that of one of his servants whose duty it is to see that they are in proper condition, or by reason of negligence on the part of those entrusted with superintendence or authorised to give the order or direction which had caused the accident; or where the accident was caused by particular orders given by a person in authority, or by defective bye-laws (provided that bye-laws should not be considered defective if authorised by the Secretary of State or Board of Trade), or by the neglect of persons in charge of signal points, a locomotive engine, or a train on a railway. But a worker could not bring an action against his employer if he or she had known of the defect or negligence which caused his accident and had failed to give notice of it to the employer or some one in authority. [Under the Common Law such a complaint has to be made to the employer in person.]

(3.) The following is a specimen form of the notice which should be sent in case of accident :—

To *Mr. John Smith, Employer,*
      Pelican Works, Battersea, S.W.
   Sir,
         Please take notice that on the *1st July, 1898, Charles Jones,* *of 250, Susan Street, Lambeth,* a $\left\{ \begin{array}{c} workman \\ workwoman \end{array} \right\}$ in your employ-ment was $\left\{ \begin{array}{c} injured \\ or\ killed \end{array} \right\}$ by *a fall from a scaffold, or by having his hand crushed in a machine, or by a sack of corn falling upon him* [as the case may be] *from which he has died.*

                                        Yours truly,
   2nd July, 1898.   *Sarah Jones.*

(4.) "Factory" has the same meaning as in the Factory and Workshop Acts, 1878-1891. It also includes any dock, wharf, quay, warehouse, machinery, or plant, to which any provision of the Acts is applied by the Act of 1895, and every laundry in which steam, water, or other mechanical power is used.

(5.) The Workmen's Compensation Act does not place all arbitrators on an equal footing. The County Court Judge and arbi-trator appointed by him alone have power to oblige witnesses to attend or to compel the production of documents. An arbitrator can refer a point of law to a County Court Judge, whose judgment would be final unless either party appealed to the Court of Appeal. This would be so if the County Court Judge were himself arbitrator. There can be no appeal against the judgment of other arbitrators if they had not referred a point of law to the County Court Judge.

(6.) Dependents are—in England, Ireland and Wales—the wife, husband, parents, grandparents, step-parents, children, grandchildren and step-children of the deceased. In Scotland the collateral rela-tives are not regarded as dependents with the husband, wife, parents and children. The mother of an illegitimate child can, however, recover damages, which is not the case in England, Ireland and Wales.

INDEX.

Industrial Law Committee

For the Enforcement of the Law and the promotion of further Reform.

Mrs. H. J. TENNANT (Chairman).
The Hon. Mrs. EDWARD TALBOT.
The Hon. Mrs. ALFRED LYTTELTON.
Mrs. HALLAM MURRAY.
Miss de CHAUMONT.
Miss GERTRUDE TUCKWELL (Hon. Secretary).

(Mrs. H. J. Tennant, formerly H.M. Superintending Inspector of Factories, and Miss de Chaumont, Sanitary Inspector, have expert experience.)

Office:
29, GREAT JAMES STREET, BEDFORD ROW, W.C. (Second Floor).

Secretary: Office Hours:
Miss WILSON.   2-30 to 3-30 (Saturdays excepted).

OBJECTS.

1.—To supply information as to the legal protection of the Industrial Classes with regard to the conditions of their trade. This information to be given by means of correspondence, lectures and printed matter, to persons working among the Industrial Classes to be used as a means of securing the observance of the law.

2.—To constitute a Central body to which may be reported breaches of the law, and other matters relating to Industrial employment, in order that these may be enquired into, referred to the proper authorities, and otherwise treated as may be deemed advisable.

3.—To consider all information received ; to promote further legislation and the more effective administration of the existing law.

Mrs. H. J. TENNANT, Chairman of the Committee, will be at home from four to six on Tuesdays at 33, Bruton Street, Berkeley Square, except during the Parliamentary Recess, in order to see any of those persons who wish for a personal interview and advice as to the best means of carrying on the work.

Lectures, delivered for the Committee by H.M. Women Inspectors of Factories, can be obtained from the Secretary, price 1d. each, or 9d. per doz. or, bound 1½d. each, or 1s. per doz.

www.ingramcontent.com/pod-product-compliance
Lightning Source LLC
Chambersburg PA
CBHW020331090426
42735CB00009B/1490